EXHAUSTED, CONFUSED AND TICKED OFF!

Hope for a New Beginning
When Change Has Done You In

by

Barbara A. Glanz, CSP, CPAE

Foreword by Ken Blanchard

TELEMACHUS PRESS

WHAT PEOPLE ARE SAYING ABOUT

EXHAUSTED CONFUSED AND TICKED OFF!

"Change is that word we often wish others would do, but we run from ourselves. Yet change is a constant part of life and business, and we need to embrace it and lean into it. How we respond to change is our choice. Barbara's book *EXHAUSTED, CONFUSED AND TICKED OFF!* guides us to consider the options and make the best choices; letting go of 'what was' to enjoy 'what can be.' Each of us gets to decide how we respond, so make the most of it! Filled with examples and useful ideas, this book can guide your attitude around facing and addressing change for the rest of your life."

—Arlin Sorenson,
VP Ecosystem, ConnectWise

"*EXHAUSTED, CONFUSED AND TICKED OFF! Hope for a New Beginning When Change Has Done You In*—Amazing title that alone touches each of us after a year of a Pandemic and the accelerated changes and huge losses that we have all faced. Finally, a book to face reality and present HOPE in ways that we can grasp, comprehend, and incorporate. One of the BEST BOOKS you could possibly read and share with family and friends!"

—Naomi Rhode, CSP, CPAE
Past President National Speakers Association
Co-Founder of Smart Practice

"Who doesn't feel overwhelmed these days? This book not only shows how to survive but find a way forward that will make you a better, stronger person. You will learn to embrace change knowing the blessings it can bring."

—Jeff Fendley,
Human Resources, Walgreens

"Whenever I hear Barbara Glanz speak or read her books, I appreciate Barbara's gift of making me stop amid the hustle and bustle of life and take the time to think and reflect on my life, my relationships and how to make them better. Barbara has done it again with *EXHAUSTED, CONFUSED AND TICKED OFF! Hope for a New Beginning When Change Has Done You In.*

"This short book is chockful of great wisdom and valuable insights on how to cope with and move forward after life-altering disruptions. And Barbara is just the writer to address these types of challenges—because she has lived through her own devastating personal losses, figured out how to overcome them and flourish.

"If there is a role model for dealing with disruptive change, Barbara Glanz is it, and *EXHAUSTED, CONFUSED AND TICKED OFF!* is worth reading. I've already read most of it twice! She has touched me again. What a gift!"

—Matt Walsh, Editor, CEO and Owner,
Observer Media Group

"Barbara points out in her new book, *EXHAUSTED, CONFUSED AND TICKED OFF!*, change is inevitable. How we navigate change is critical, and having the understanding and the tools to make good choices will ultimately provide us with more hope and joy in our lives.

"And, as Barbara so convincingly states, when we truly learn to embrace change, we can fully experience the gifts that go along with it. I hope all of you will appreciate Barbara's wisdom in this new book as much as I do."

—Steven J. Cochlan,
Founder, ALS Family of Faith

"This book is exactly like its author: Short, delightful, insightful, sexy, wise, kind, helpful, and loving. Allow them both to speak into your life."

—Randy Gage,
Author on the international bestseller, *Radical Rebirth*

"Most people struggle with change. Real change. The soil of our lives becomes packed solid with routines, obligations and expectations that can keep us stuck in the illusion of comfort and certainty. Then, much like an unwanted gift, a once-in-a-lifetime circumstance as profound as a widespread pandemic comes. Yet, just in time, Barbara Glanz comes along with many ideas that will move you forward. As you read what Barbara has shared and discover the GIFTS in change, you will find yourself REFRESHED, CLEAR and JOYFUL."

—John G. Blumberg,
Author of *Return On Integrity:*
The Individual's Journey to the One Essential Thing

"Every human on our planet is aware that change is a constant in our lives. Some of that change is what we seek, but some changes hit us out of the blue. Barbara Glanz speaks firsthand when it comes to change that is thrust upon us as she has experienced heartbreaking events in her life that would have done in the strongest of our species. But she put those traumatic changes in her life in perspective and was able to work through them and emerge a stronger person.

"When change happens, whether it's the good, the bad, or the ugly, Barbara clarifies that we always have a choice. We can become bitter and continue to dwell in the past or seek a new beginning. Barbara provides a living, breathing practical guide to working through the trauma of change to find the gifts in all changes in our lives."

**—Dan Steininger, JD,
CLU, Retired CEO of a major financial institution**

"Barbara has an Angelic ability to share personal experiences that Inspire us to see the gifts that we can find in change. This book is a simple, yet very powerful roadmap to deal with change in a proactive way."

**—Jeff Strong, CEO,
Strong's Marine**

"In *EXHAUSTED, CONFUSED AND TICKED OFF!*, Barbara Glanz lays out the *PERFECT* blueprint to help you manage the struggles associated with the life change (and transform them into growth)—this is a must read!"

—Daniel Deems, MD, PhD–Neuroscientist

"True to form, Barbara once again distills a complex issue into an easy to understand concept with this book. Change is a constant in our lives and as Barbara points out we have a choice in how we respond to that constant. Valuing change as a gift and opportunity inspires innovation, allowing us to ultimately become better individuals, employees and business leaders."

**—William (Bill) Stoller, CEO and Co-Founder,
Express Employment Professionals**

DEDICATION

To all of us who have faced difficult change and found our way back to a new beginning … again and again and again.

And especially to my beautiful granddaughter, Kinsey, who has been a role model of bravery, strength, and always positive thinking as she has battled leukemia and all the consequences since she was 15. She has taught us all how to move forward and find joy, even in the midst of difficult times.

What the caterpillar calls the end of the world,
the Master calls the butterfly.

Your deepest struggle can, if you're willing and open,
produce your greatest strength.
~Oprah Winfrey

EXHAUSTED, CONFUSED AND TICKED OFF!

Hope for a New Beginning When Change Has Done You In

FOREWORD

I am a raving fan of Barbara Glanz! She is a lifetime learner who is willing to share her learnings and vulnerability with anyone who wants to improve their life. Her latest book, "EXHAUSTED, CONFUSED AND TICKED OFF!: Hope for a New Beginning When Change Has Done You In!" is one of her very best. After this Covid 19 pandemic, if change hasn't "done you in" in one way or another, you probably fib about other things too!

> *Suffering and change are a part of life. We spend well over 50% of our lives today in change. "Transition" has become the norm and "stability" the exception.*
>
> ~James R. Zullo

Benjamin Franklin once said that the only two things we can count on to be never changing are death and taxes! Today I think we would all add a third—change itself.

Almost no one likes change … yet we cannot avoid it, so we must learn to deal with it and not lose our hearts and minds. Even in the midst of the most difficult changes, we all need HOPE that there can be a "new beginning". Charles Darwin wrote many years ago, "it's not the strongest of the species that survives, not the most intelligent, but the one most responsive to change."

Read Barbara Glanz's wonderful book about Change and Choice to move on—to understand the process of change, to discover new tools for coping with change, and ultimately to find the gifts which every change can hold.

—Ken Blanchard,
Co-Author of the *One Minute Manager*
and *Servant Leadership in Action*

INTRODUCTION
"Setting the Stage"

In 2002 a new speaker colleague of mine and I found that we each had lost a child. His loss was more recent than mine, but I had just lost my husband of 34 years, so we were united in our suffering. Over the many months of healing, as we talked about both our business and our personal losses, we decided to use our struggle and subsequent growth to help others who were facing similar circumstances. As a result, we began to design a workshop about how to understand and succeed through change.

Although the workshop was powerful, it was very difficult to market at that time, so we both put it aside. Several years ago, I was asked to do a keynote on Change for the National Convention of the Society for Human Resource Management, so I took parts of the workshop, added models I had created in my other work as well as some new material, and I presented the workshop at their international convention. I got wonderful feedback, but since I had already established a brand of "Spreading Contagious Enthusiasm™" which focused mainly on customer service and employee engagement, I again put the Change presentation aside.

Over the next few years I did the new Change presentation as a keynote speech several times when my customers requested it, but I continued my brand of "Spreading Contagious Enthusiasm™" for the majority of my work. About four years ago I became convinced by the current climate and my clients' feedback that they needed inspiration and tools to create workplaces of kindness. As a result, that became my major focus with a presentation titled, "Is Incivility the New Norm? Creating a Culture of Kindness," and Change again went on the back burner.

Finally, last year many of my clients began requesting a presentation on dealing with Change—and then Covid 19 hit! I became convinced without a doubt that this was the right time for this book. Since we will all be going through change for the rest of our lives, the ideas in the book will not only help you discover a new understanding of the process of change but will also give you many helpful ideas for coping skills to encourage you through the journey.

When I speak on this topic around the world, I always ask the audience members to write down at the very beginning, "**All change comes bearing gifts**." And again, at the end of our time together. I refer them back to this powerful and life-changing thought.

I have realized through the many changes in my own life that this statement is absolutely true—we just have to be willing to look for those gifts. The Chinese symbol for change has two lines connecting to each other. One line is the symbol for "danger" and the other is the one for "opportunity." How we respond depends on which one we focus on.

A famous Chinese proverb says. "**The beginning of wisdom is UNDERSTANDING**," and that is what I want to tackle in this short book. I can never take the pain away from the changes you are experiencing, but by beginning to understand where you are in the process in a clear and simple way, you will be better equipped to navigate through those troubled waters and come out on the other side a wiser and hopefully more compassionate human being.

The only way that we can live, is if we grow. The only way that we can grow, is if we change. The only way that we can change, is if we are willing to learn.

~Anonymous

Finally, I hope these ideas will help you learn to find the gifts in change rather than being mired in the past. I am honored to travel this tumultuous journey to understanding and new beginnings with you.

Blessings,

Chapter One:
FINDING THE GIFTS IN EVERY STAGE OF CHANGE

CHANGE IS HARD! The pandemic, job losses, working from home, homeschooling, violent protests, devastating fires, hurricanes and floods, and the whole political scene are causing stress, overwhelming anxiety, fear, and a lack of focus in our world today.

Change comes into our lives and unmoors us from our secure foundations and propels us from our comfort zones. We are forced to stretch, to learn new things, to let go of the "old" ways. We often come kicking and screaming to accepting pain and growing with change, but we CAN do it. We have to mourn and feel the pain, but then it is our choice to move on, and with that choice can come amazing gifts.

There are many kinds of change—personal, organizational, technological and societal, and certainly, change has become the status quo in most of the world today. Each person has to go through his or her own transition process, and each person will deal with the changes in their lives a little differently. However, there is a fundamental process that occurs in all change that will help you find understanding, acceptance and finally the gifts from those changes in every stage of the process, both in your organizational and in your personal life.

Helen Keller talked about how when God closes a door (change), He always opens a window, but we spend so much time looking at the closed door (the past), that we often don't even see the window (new beginning) that has been opened for us! When we choose to look for those growth opportunities, we begin to see the gifts that change can bring to our lives.

It is your CHOICE!

We choose change OR it chooses us. Change can be the most exciting thing that happens, and it's the only way you'll grow as a person.
~Anonymous

An interesting phenomenon I see in my work worldwide is that most people do not understand that no matter what happens to them, they always have choices in how they respond. Instead, they feel victimized and try to find solace in blame and excuses. One of the greatest gifts I can give you in this book is to help you understand and apply the choices you have in any change so you no longer have to be a victim. Instead, at different points in the process, you will be free to discover the gifts that change has brought.

When I first started speaking, I created this three-column chart to help me measure the difference I could make in every interaction. However, it also applies to our choices during any kind of change in our lives. If we allow the change to completely overwhelm us, it is a minus. We are stuck in the past. If we simply ignore the change, minimize it, or bury it in our sub-conscious, we have done nothing to handle the change and learn from it, so it is a zero (Survival Only).

However, if we realize the change CAN result in positives and ultimately new learnings, we are moving forward to a new beginning (Acceptance and Growth).

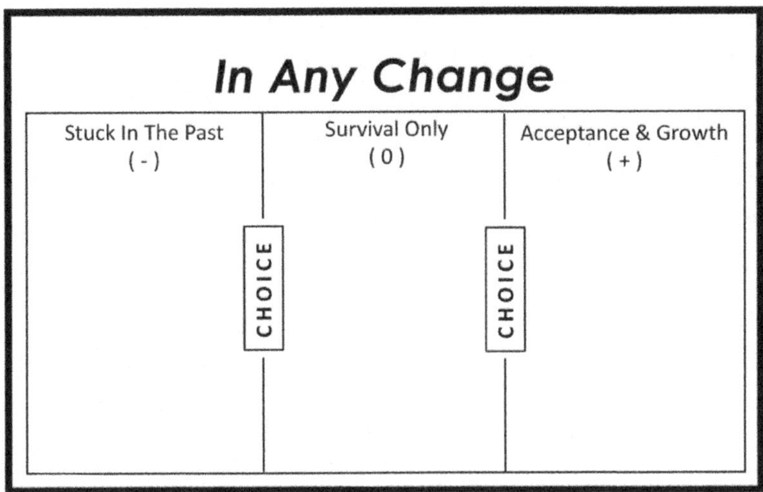

When I speak about choices, I often tell the story of two of my husband's friends who commuted to downtown Chicago together for nineteen years. They always took the same train and stopped at the same newsstand for the paper every day, five days a week.

Every morning one of the friends would say to the man at the newsstand, "HI, Joe! How are you today? How's your family? What did you think of the Cubs this weekend?" and other small talk. Never once, however, in all those nineteen years did Joe ever learn his name or respond to him in any other way than a grunt.

Finally, my husband's friend said, "How can you be nice to this guy day after day when he doesn't even acknowledge your presence on the face of the earth?" I will never forget his response. He said, "You know, I learned a long time ago not to let someone else control my behavior."

This story has served me well as I have faced many changes in my life. What it says to me is that no matter what anyone says or does to me or no matter what changes occur in my life, I ALWAYS have a choice in how I respond. That thought is one of the most empowering lessons I have ever learned in my life. No matter how hard a change may be for us, we each have the ability to choose HOW we are going to respond. It may not be easy, but we can either end up being better or bitter!

When we apply this model to what is happening to each of us in the changes in our lives, there are really just three choices. If we constantly complain, focus on all the losses, allow ourselves to feel completely overwhelmed, or even give up to ongoing depression, we remain stuck in the past, choosing the negative (-).

If we find ourselves simply surviving with little hope and little joy, robotlike, we are stuck in the struggle, the middle of the transition, and there is no growth or learning (0).

However, if we try to find the good in this "new normal," continue to learn new ways of coping, and accept that "this is the way it is," we have begun to embrace the change (+). Certainly, we will waver from time to time, yet ultimately it is our CHOICE to determine our attitude toward the change and begin to move toward acceptance and a new beginning.

Two Levels of Any Situation

In any circumstance there are always two levels, the Business level (the facts) and the Human level (our emotions). We need to keep these in mind as we work through any change, especially the pandemic of 2020.

On the Business level, we need to follow all the "requirements"—wearing masks, washing our hands, social distancing, taking care of ourselves. However, the most important part of moving through this transition is acknowledging and dealing with our feelings, the Human level.

During any transition like grieving (and we really are grieving "the way things were"), we will experience feelings of fear, anger, loneliness and depression. Burying these feelings will only keep us stuck, so we must find healthy ways to cope with them. In a later chapter I will share many different ideas to do just that. These were the gifts I found in my journey through change.

Chapter Two:
MY STORY

EVEN BEFORE THE pandemic of 2020, I had become an expert on change! On the business level after being a stay-at-home Mom for 19 years, I returned to the workforce when I was 45 years old. Over the years, I have been downsized, I have lost a job, I have started my own company, I have had three different careers, and I have experienced huge technological changes. I have had several changes in location, I have traveled the world and experienced many different cultures, and I have managed (often not too well) eight different assistants!

On the personal side, I have raised three children who now all live far away, I have had heath issues, I have lost a child, and my husband of 34 years died of cancer at a young age. At age 56, I had lost my father, my son, and my husband, not how I planned my life to be. After my husband's death, I moved from Illinois to Florida where I knew no one, and the weirdest change of all was to start dating again in my 60s!

Many of these changes were forced upon me and terribly painful, and some took a very long time (several years) before I could finally move forward with HOPE. Other changes, even though planned, were still difficult. Yet, as a result, I learned life lessons that have served me well over the years, and I will share these with you in a later chapter. Best of all, I have learned firsthand that "All change really does come bearing gifts," even though some may take a long time to realize.

Chapter Three:
THE CHANGE MODEL

ONE OF MY gifts as a speaker and writer is to take complex ideas and distill them into simple visual models as you have seen earlier in the book. Since most of us today are visual learners, this has become a profound way to explore difficult concepts. As I was going through the heartbreaking change of losing my husband, I worked with my friend who had also had a major loss in his life, and with his very valuable input, I created this new model of change.

As you remember, the Chinese proverb says, "The beginning of wisdom is understanding," so this model will help you visually understand where you are in the change process and help you more clearly see your way to a new beginning.

As I said earlier, "Change is HARD!" and this model cannot take the pain of change away, but it will help you become aware of what you have to do to get through the transition in a more positive, conscious and hopeful way … to finally accepting and embracing the change in order to move on with your life and find the gifts that change has brought.

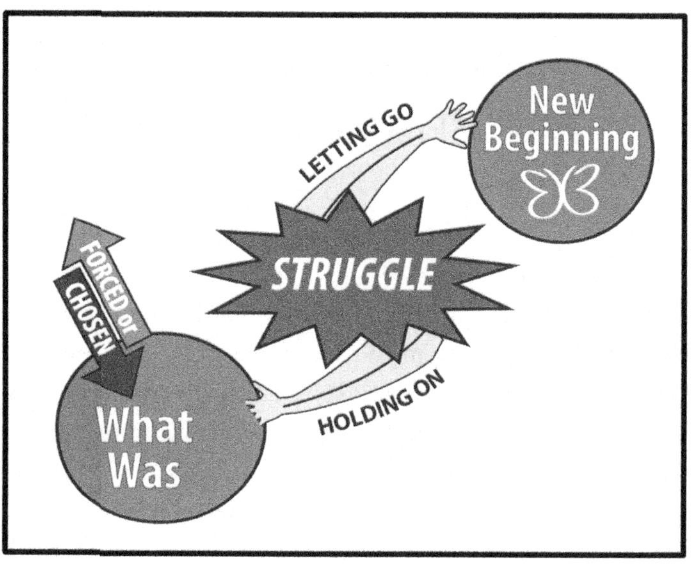

CHANGE MODEL

Part One: "What Was"

Every change begins with "What Was," the way things were before the change occurred. Unfortunately, many people get stuck in this stage and never move away from it. In order to move forward, we need to identify the "what was" in our own transition. When my husband died, for example, "What Was" was that I was a wife, part of a couple, and the life partner of a lovely man for 34 years, nearly my whole adult life. All of a sudden, I was alone! After we identify the "what was," only then can we begin the very difficult process of letting go, another stage in the change process.

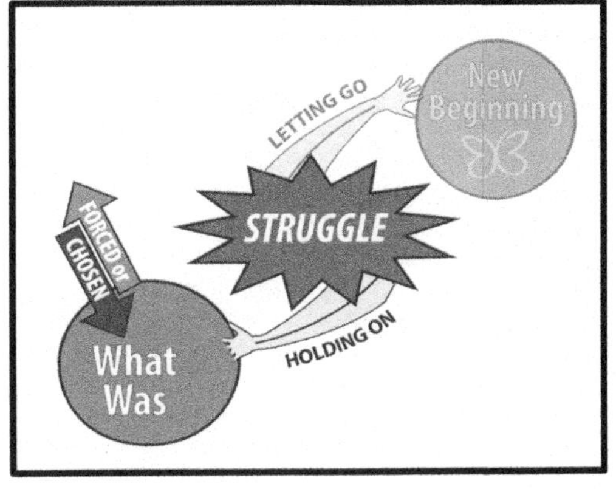

Chapter Four:
KINDS OF CHANGE

LIKE THE PANDEMIC, the lightning bolt of change can come out of nowhere and brutally force us out of our normal life (what was) with little or no preparation. There are other changes that we may plan, such as a move, having a child, a promotion, or taking a new job. However, even in a positive planned change, we will still experience a transition, and some are much more difficult than others. When we understand the four kinds of change, we discover a kind of continuum for the changes that have happened in our lives.

1. Predictable or Unexpected

Some changes in our lives are predictable and some are completely unexpected. The hardest ones to deal with, of course, are the changes that are unexpected. In my case, I had had a completely normal pregnancy with our second child, so his death, especially since I had not even taken an aspirin during the pregnancy and the whole birth process was completely normal, was really unexpected and sudden.

As you go through the change process, think about whether the change you are experiencing was predictable or unexpected. The pandemic, for example, was completely unexpected which results in a much more difficult transition. Yet even with predictable changes, we still have to go through a stressful transition period which we will discuss next.

2. Forced or Chosen

Some changes are changes we choose such as getting married, having children, starting a new job, moving to a new home or location, or even retiring. Yet we still must go through the transition from what was to a new beginning. Other changes, like my earlier examples, are forced upon us, such as the death of someone we love, health fears, losing a job, going through a divorce, or being forced to make a move for the organization.

Now think about your current situation—was it forced or was it chosen? Again, with the current pandemic, it was forced upon us.

When we look at change on a continuum, the easiest kind of change is Chosen and Predictable because we have made the decision that we WANT the change to occur. However, there will still be difficulties to work through, especially emotionally, when that change happens.

For example, in business when we get a promotion, we have to face that our relationships with our peers will be different, our responsibilities will be greater, and we might have a steep learning curve rather than a secure comfort level about our work.

In our personal lives when we make a chosen move to a new location (think retirement for many), we leave friends and family, we leave familiar places to shop and eat, and we leave doctors and dentists and other support givers. Even when we become empty nesters, our lifestyle changes (no more sports or concerts to attend at the schools, no more carpooling, no more staying up late to enforce curfews!). Our relationships with each of our family members changes as our children become adults, and we may even have to "re-find" our marriage partners now that we finally have alone time together. So even "positive" changes can be stressful.

Of course, the most difficult transitions of all are those that are forced and unpredictable. We are immediately thrown into a maelstrom of grief and fear, not knowing what the future might bring. These transitions may take months or even years to accept. When our little boy died and was buried on Christmas Eve, it took me several years before I could fully enjoy Christmas again. I struggled with seeing any babies or toddlers for many months, and some days I could not even think about getting out of bed! However, as I finally began to accept that change, I learned some life lessons that I will share later in the book, and this becomes the "new beginning," filled with gifts that we may never have learned without the pain of change.

CHANGE MODEL

Part Two: "The Struggle"

It's not that people are afraid of change or so in love with their old ways, but it's the place in between that people fear. It's like Linus when his blanket is in the dryer. He has nothing to hold on to.

~Charles Schulz

I have chosen to call the part of change when we begin to face what has happened as the "Struggle." This stage of change has many different names—the transition, the dark night of the soul, chaos, a passage. However, for me, the Struggle is the most accurate name because it reflects the devastating process of

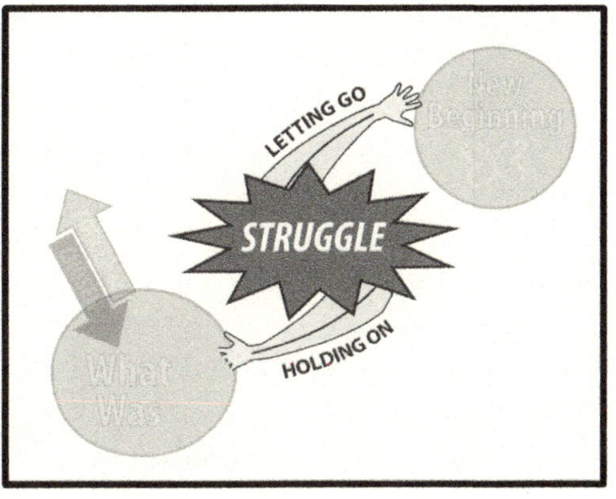

trying to find some deeper meaning and purpose in order to be able to go on with your life. It is the hardest thing any of us will ever have to do … yet the good news is that you CAN get through anything with enough time, understanding, self-compassion, and support. In a later section of the book, we will discuss some concrete ways to navigate this awful struggle.

> *The bottom line is to trust the processes of change and trust that transition is God's way of helping you become all that you were created to be.*
>
> ~James R. Zullo

Chapter Five:
PHASES OF THE STRUGGLE PROCESS

YOU WILL PROBABLY go through all of these stages as you work through the changes in your life. However, the more serious the change (Forced and Unpredictable), the longer it may take you in any of the stages, especially Confusion. However, just identifying where you are today will help you move to the next stage.

1. Denial—At this point in the struggle we often are in shock and barely surviving. When our little boy died, my immediate reaction was one of, "This really can't be happening to me. I had a completely normal pregnancy—I never even took an aspirin. They must have made some mistake!" I remember so many days violently waking up after just a couple of hours of sleep and thinking, "Thank God, it was all just a bad dream." Yet, of course, it wasn't.

Emotionally, we cannot accept the reality of what has happened, so it is easier to just rationalize and pretend in order to save our sanity. During this phase, you almost want to check out of the world, so staying in bed all day is one way of coping for many. In this phase we still are having difficulty accepting the reality of the change. People often experience changes in physical health, emotional balance, logical thinking patterns, and normal behavior patterns.

2. Resistance—This is the stage when we often get angry, and we want to blame someone or something. Depression, frustration, anger, rage, envy, guilt, and resentment become visible. For example, many people whose loved ones have died believe it was the fault of the doctor or the hospital, and they get caught up in lawsuits and can spend a long time in this stage. However, different people respond differently in this stage. My reaction was to dwell on shame and guilt—what might I have done to cause my baby to die? In this stage it is critically important to admit and acknowledge your feelings. Otherwise, you can get stuck here.

3. Confusion—This is usually the longest and most difficult stage of the Struggle for most of us. Sadly, some people get stuck here and never seem able to accept what has happened and move on with their lives. No energy, feelings of nothingness, powerlessness, loss of identity and direction, no sense of grounding or meaning often occur in this phase. There can be a breakdown of value systems and beliefs. Some even question their faith if they are Believers—"Where is God in my pain?"

Defense mechanisms begin to lose usefulness and meaning, and depression follows. We question, WHY? "When other people had healthy babies all the time, WHY did MY child have to die?" We are struggling for answers when there usually are none. We want some kind of closure. How are we going to go on with our lives? Will things ever be the same again? In my case, I could not stand to go back to my doctor's office when there would be many pregnant women and babies there. I could not imagine ever going to a baby shower again, and I avoided anyone who had children. Many days I feared I could not even get through until noon, let alone a whole day.

For many, depending on the seriousness and depth of the change, this phase can take several months or sometimes years to work through. I learned how important it is to be gentle with yourself during this phase and not to listen to other's expectations, but to honor your own feelings. Rushing this phase in order to please others can result in many extra years of struggle.

CHANGE MODEL

Part Three: "Stages of
The New Beginning"

As we begin the healing process, we are moving toward acceptance and a new perspective on our lives. We are beginning to see some of the gifts in the change.

1. Exploration—In this stage we begin to feel some resignation and to passively begin to accept the change, though usually without any enthusiasm. This is really the first step towards the New Beginning, and often the most personal growth happens in this phase. It becomes a time of openness and even readiness to think about new ways of approaching one's life. This can also be a time of great creativity. Interestingly, when one hits rock bottom, there is a greater tendency to risk because no threat is greater than the pain one is already feeling.

During this phase, for example, I began to be more comfortable about being around other people with babies and young children. Others that I didn't even know came forward and shared their losses with me. I began learning more about what had happened and started to think about having another child. Healing was beginning.

When I lost my job, I at last had the courage to take the risk to start my own company because I realized I could always find another job. I was beginning to realize the GIFTS of change!

> *In order for us to move from one place to another—to step outside the lines of our lives and grow—we must embrace change. For us to grow, we must look at things in a new light.*
>
> ~Robert Ismon Brown

2. Commitment—Finally, in this phase we feel that we CAN go on with our lives and one of the beautiful results is that we usually find a way to make something good come from our experience of loss and pain. Rechanneled energy results in positive changes and a return to some semblance of "normal" life with a deeper understanding and purpose.

I learned, for example, that I could counsel and comfort other people who had lost children and walk beside them on their journey. After several years, I was asked to be interviewed for a new organization called "Compassionate Friends" which was founded to support parents who had lost a child of any age. This group and its newsletter brought me a great deal of comfort. Finally, I was able to share my experience and growth with others who were hurting. Ultimately, I even wrote a book called "What Can I Do!? Ideas to Help Those Who Have Experienced a Loss." I was able to finally find the gifts in this change.

Chapter Six:
SURVIVING THE STRUGGLE
Victim or Survivor?

Courage is not the absence of despair and fear but the capacity to move ahead in spite of them.

~James R. Zullo

In every loss exists an opportunity for you to transform somehow ... for you to grow through it.

DURING THE PERIOD of the Struggle, we all need to have ways to help us cope with the dark place where we find ourselves. Everyone will find different ways to navigate this journey, so there are no right or wrong ways. However, I want to share some of the things that have helped me.

1. DAILY COPING TOOLS

- During my time of terrible grieving, a friend sent me a book titled, "I Ain't Much, Baby, But I'm All I've Got!" This book had a profound effect on me at that time. The author, who had had devastating changes and struggles of his own, talked about learning **to live five minutes at a time**. This practice, in many ways, was what saved me during my deepest depression and ultimately became a lifelong gift to me. On so many days when I couldn't even think ahead a couple of hours, I could always get through five minutes … just five more minutes, and five more. It was a way of survival at that time, but more importantly it taught me to be FULLY in the present at all times. When I am with you, I am totally with you, not thinking about anyone or anything else. We now call this Mindfulness. That has been one of the greatest life lessons I have ever learned—and it all came out of my pain!

- **Live life one day at a time**. As I worked through some of the stages of grieving, I finally could get beyond living five minutes, and I began to live just one day at a time. We cannot change the past, and we may only have this very day to make a difference, so I learned to simply deal with the immediate issues within my control at that moment and not worry about tomorrow. In fact, I could often not even "see" tomorrow during the survival part of the struggle, but I knew I had moved forward when I could at least think about getting through an entire day.

- I also learned that **every day is a gift**. No matter what has happened, now I thank God when I wake up every morning. My losses have taught me what a privilege it is to be alive, and we never know what surprises the day may hold for us. For example, I always choose a word or phrase that becomes a theme for each new year. One of my favorites has been, "Surprise me again, Lord!" I loved looking all day for those many surprises, even though some were not ones I would have chosen! We don't know how much time we have left, so we need to celebrate each and every day.

- **Keep a "Blessings" journal**. During any kind of change, it helps to focus on what is going right rather than what is going wrong. When we take time to put good things in writing, we begin to see more clearly the blessings that occur in our lives each day. Every day I write down 2 or 3 things that happened that day that were a blessing to me. I have found that even on the very worst days of my life, I can still always find a moment or two of blessing. It facilitates healing to focus on what is going right instead of what is going wrong, and keeping a blessings journal not only helps one focus on the positives but also helps that process become a habit.

- **Have some quiet time each day.** When we find ourselves in the struggle of grieving, it is important to connect with our core. What are the values or foundation that our life is built upon? For some it is a faith orientation and for others it may be a belief in self or nature, but whatever it is, we need quiet, reflective time to "re-find" our center. I suggest committing to either a few minutes in the early morning or just before going to bed at night when our lives are more relaxed. Deep breathing and simply sitting in silence can help one find some peace in the midst of struggle. Meditation and Mindfulness are even being taught online if we might need a more structured approach. Some helpful apps are Calm, Insight Timer, Health, Headspace, and Planet Fitness.

- **Keep a diary or a journal**. A good way to acknowledge what you are thinking or feeling in a concrete way is to write it down. For example, I often write letters to God, and they become a kind of prayer as well as a way for me to let things go. Never write for anyone except yourself and never worry about spelling or punctuation—just simply write. I write when I am happy, angry, worried, confused, or in pain about something. I also tape things in my journal that bring me joy or make me think. Not only does writing become a catharsis, but when I go back sometimes weeks or months later and read what I have written, I realize how far I have come in my healing, another precious gift.

Reminder Checklist:

- Live five minutes at a time.
- Just take one day at a time.
- Remember every day is a gift.
- Keep a blessings journal.
- Have some quiet time each day.
- Keep a diary or a journal.

To download the checklists and other information, go to:

https://barbaraglanz.com/book-extras

2. GIVE YOURSELF PERMISSION FOR SELF-CARE

- **Be gentle to yourself**. Especially during the first few weeks and months and sometimes years of our grieving, we need to be kind to ourselves. We need to let go of other's expectations and many times their advice and find what works just for us. I will never forget when after our baby died, a young pastor came by for a visit several weeks later, and he literally chastised me for not "getting on with my life." I realize now that he could never have understood the pain I was in, but his statement set me back many weeks since it made me feel guilty and shamed. During any kind of change, one MUST hold onto a belief in oneself and not allow anyone else's judgment to pull you down. Be proud of baby steps!

- I learned that **I would always be true to myself**. Because I was hurting so deeply, I realized that no one could ever hurt me that much again, so I vowed I would never "play games" with anyone again. I will ALWAYS be authentically myself.

- **Give yourself permission to have fun**. I remember how hard it was to laugh for many months in the midst of my pain, and even when I did, I felt guilty. However, I learned that as research shows, laughter is good for not only our health but also for our soul. When you feel more comfortable, try to watch funny movies, read humorous books, choose to be with people who make you laugh. One of my friends has a newsletter called "Laughing Matters." You can subscribe to it at https://humorproject.com/.

Again, when you are ready, plan special outings with friends for lunch or dinner, for a play or movie, or for a special shopping trip, anything that brings you comfort and some joy.

- **Watch and read things that bring YOU joy.** In the midst of difficult times, we need more than ever to find moments of joy. These will be different for everyone since we all have different interests and tastes. Some people find escape in action movies and books, others with romance or good human-interest stories, some with documentaries and travel, and others from more spiritual writing. Netflix has been a blessing for many during this pandemic when we are not able to go out. There are some wonderful thought-provoking documentaries as well as heartwarming series that we can "binge" on when we need a break from the reality of our lives. Again, give yourself permission to watch and read whatever adds joy to your life.

- **Plan to be with people you love or want to get to know better.** Choose wisely whom you spend time with during this period of struggle. There is a wonderful quotation that says whenever we interact with anyone, it leaves both us and the other person on a higher or a lower plane. I ask my audiences, "Aren't there people in your life who just suck the energy right out of you whenever you are around them? And then aren't there people who make you feel like you can conquer the world? Which people do you want to spend time with and which one do YOU want to be?"

When we are hurting, we need to give ourselves permission to choose to not be around toxic people. In both our personal and professional lives, we may not have the choice to totally avoid them, but we always have the choice to not allow them to change us and our feelings. That is difficult, but as we get stronger, we can learn to see these people with compassion and let their words go. I love what Lou Holtz says, "Why is it that the people who need love and understanding the most usually deserve it the least?" They, too, have a story!

- **Find an exercise you enjoy.** Research shows that when we move our bodies, we release endorphins that lift our spirits. Often when we are in the struggle, we find ourselves lethargic and without energy, so it is hard to want to do any kind of exercise. But we need to be gentle with ourselves and start small. Even a short walk around the block is a beginning. Try some different things that work best for you. I am a swimmer, so when I was in the depths of grieving, I made myself go to the pool every day during adult swim. It was the only time I did not think—I just counted my laps.

When I lived in Illinois, I could not swim in the winter, so I purchased a used treadmill and to this day, when I can't find time to do anything else, I can always do a few minutes on it. It is amazing the difference you feel when you simply move! It is also important to get enough sleep and eat a well-balanced and healthy diet, yet both are difficult in the midst of the struggle. Many days I did not want to get out of bed, and I had no appetite. When I made myself do something physical, however, I began to eat and sleep better.

Reminder Checklist:

- Be gentle to yourself.
- Always be true to yourself.
- Give yourself permission to have fun.
- Watch and read things that bring you joy.
- Plan to be with people you love or want to get to know better.
- Find an exercise you enjoy.

To download the checklists and other information, go to:

https://barbaraglanz.com/book-extras

3. FOCUS ON OTHERS

- **Appreciate others.** One of the best ways to get out of our own despair is to focus on others. Again, this is not easy, but if we start with noticing small things that people do for us and appreciating them for it, it will move our focus from ourselves to thinking about others. I love that appreciation is a FREE gift—it costs us nothing except a bit of awareness. And it always makes one feel better to see the effect it has on people—very often they are surprised that someone even noticed.

  A recent HR study found that 65% of American workers said they got NO appreciation for their good work all last year. Whether in your personal or professional life, one of the easiest ways to cope with devastating change is to take your focus away from your own pain and begin to appreciate others around you. You will be giving a gift, both to them AND to yourself!

- **Join a support group.** This is one of the most important coping mechanisms during the struggle. It is often difficult to take the first step to go to a group; however, now we can find almost any kind of support group online. It is much easier to be anonymous until we feel comfortable in sharing. Finding others who are in similar circumstances helps us to realize we are not alone, and we can learn from their sharing and experiences as well as ask for their help. I have always loved the thought from C.S. Lewis, "What? You, too? I thought I was the only one."

  When our little boy died, I found great comfort simply in the newsletters sent by Compassionate Friends and Bereaved Parents of the USA, both organizations for those who have lost a child of any age. When my husband died, I attended a

Grief group at my church. Not only did these groups help me find new ways of coping, but I was also able to help some others as time went on.

In my professional life, when I was let go from a job I had developed and loved, I found support through others in my profession who had had similar situations and empathized with me as well as giving me ideas and encouragement. Today we can find support for what is happening with the pandemic in many different publications, in our houses of worship, and with friends and families who are going through the same difficulties. We just need to learn to ASK for help! And then, as we learn and grow in acceptance, we can begin to focus on others and be there for them as they struggle through their own pain.

- **Have compassion for others.** As I said earlier, one of the things I have learned over the years is that everyone has a story. Some stories are more difficult than others, yet for the person having the experience, it can be the darkest of times. I remember after my husband died, I had a friend who would call me and constantly complain that her husband was often late coming home from work and was not helping with putting the children to bed. Sometimes I wanted to scream, "Shut up! At least you HAVE a husband!"

However, over the years I have learned not to judge what anyone else is going through. In their mind and in their story at that time, they are in pain. No one else can really understand even if they have had a similar experience. All we can do is to listen, hold their hand, and walk beside them. Again, when we take our focus off ourselves in the later stages of the struggle and begin to focus on others, we are getting closer to acceptance and a new beginning.

We delight in the beauty of the butterfly, but rarely admit the changes it has gone through to achieve that beauty.

~Maya Angelou

Reminder checklist:

- Appreciate others.
- Join a support group.
- Have compassion for others.

To download the checklists and other information, go to:

https://barbaraglanz.com/book-extras

4. BEGIN TO SEE WITH NEW EYES

"When one road ends, it's time to look ahead in a new direction. And know that as far as your eye can see, the universe can see even farther."

~Oprah Winfrey

- **Change or modify your expectations.** Lowering your expectations for yourself and others will help you get through this time of struggle. As I said earlier, we need to be gentle with ourselves and accept that we are, in many ways, just simply surviving during this time. It is also important not to allow the expectations of others to cause you more stress and pain. NO ONE can possibly understand what you are going through, so gently remind them of that if you have to.

  During this pandemic, we have had to learn to find new ways of living our lives. Children have had to learn to go to school virtually, parents and others have had to devise a place and plan to work at home, we have had to cook at home or order in rather than going to restaurants, and all of our group and social activities have been canceled. We have had to change our expectations for what makes a "good" day and find new ways of working, entertainment, and staying in touch with friends and family. How grateful I am for Zoom when all my children and grandchildren live 3000 miles away!

- **Reframe your beliefs.** Often after a time of change, we find that things we took for granted are no longer available to us. Instead of focusing on all that we have lost, we can begin to focus on things that we still have or even the blessings to come from this experience. Changing the way we think about a situation can make it easier to bear. For example, after I was let go from my job as Director of Training, following a deep period of mourning, I began to realize that I now had the freedom to start my own company.

In the pandemic we are learning to reframe what we initially saw as something terrible to begin to see some benefits—such as cleaner air and water, more family time, healthier eating, no commute time for many, greater freedom in doing our jobs. As a professional speaker, all my scheduled work and travel for the year was cancelled, so as time went by, I began, with the help of many of my colleagues, to reframe my thinking to realize I could still reach many people virtually. I have learned Zoom, and although the rewards are not the same, my business has begun picking back up, and I am using my gifts to again bring hope to people.

- **Treasure the Good Memories.** When you are able to appreciate the precious memories from the time of "What Was" instead of the losses, you are beginning to heal. You are seeing with new eyes how blessed you were to have that person in your life or to have that special job or to have the kind of life you wanted, even if only for a short while. Focusing on those moments and gifts will help you find new strength and help you celebrate the good times rather than dwelling on the pain of loss.

  After my husband died, a friend gave me a beautiful photo album with the following quotation in the front:

  "You have been given the Gift of a very special love … a Gift that was never intended to be 'forever' … but one that will lifelong be unforgettable! Treasure the joy, the

memories, the moving reality that you have shared life and death in all of its tumultuous fullness with one of God's finest!"

She said to fill it with all my favorite pictures of Charlie and me, and then I could take it with me whenever I traveled so I would not feel alone. Today that lovely album sits on a table in my living room as a beautiful memory, not of a loss, but of a precious love.

When I lost the job I mentioned earlier, with time, I became grateful for how much I had learned there, and I was able to celebrate all the changes I brought to that department and the wonderful people I had hired and trained. Many of them are still friends today!

I have been trying to make the best of grief and am just beginning to learn to allow it to make the best of me.
~Barbara Lazear Ascher

Reminder checklist:

- Change or modify your expectations.
- Reframe your beliefs.
- Treasure the good memories.

To download the checklists and other information, go to:

https://barbaraglanz.com/book-extras

Chapter Seven:
DISCOVER NEW STRENGTHS AND OPPORTUNITIES

ONE OF THE greatest gifts to come from change is the discovery of creative new ways to handle future change as well as opportunities to help others as they, too, struggle through transitions in their lives.

- **Learn.** Read books and articles about your situation when you are ready. Talk to people who have gone through something similar. Many non-profit groups offer free counseling services. As you become more able to focus, perhaps take a class that will help you find some new direction and open new doors for discovery. One of the gifts of change is new knowledge that we can use to help ourselves and others in the future.

- **Start a 100 Day Project.** At the National Speakers Association virtual convention in July, one of the speakers was Michelle Poler who talked about her 100 day project to conquer her fears. The idea intrigued me. It is a short commitment but an important one to give us a new purpose.

Since not being able to travel and do my keynote speaking except by Zoom, I had been searching for a way to make a difference in this new world of sheltering. Over these past six months, I have received a number of emails, calls, and cards telling me how much people needed inspiration and hope and asking me to please help them stay positive. However, other than my postings on my social networking sites, I wasn't quite sure how to do that.

After thinking about this for some time, I realized that besides being a very positive person, one of my greatest strengths is being a good listener. Since I am also an encourager and a lover of people, I finally decided what my 100 day project would be:

Each day I would contact someone who has been important in my life, many whom I have not spoken with in years. I remembered the saying that people enter our lives for a reason or for a season. Then in our busyness, we often lose track of them. Thus, it became my mission in this 100 days to track down many of these people and reconnect with them.

What a delight it has been! I have found that since I made the commitment, people have come to mind (often in the middle of the night), and they are the ones I try to contact the next day. I also started a long list for my future calls. What has been most amazing is that in almost every case, the call at that time to that person has turned out to be a very special gift to us both. Two friends with whom I had not spoken for years, for example, had just found out they were facing cancer and really needed encouragement as well as my sharing how much they had meant to me.

I spoke with a number of clients who had hired me 15–20 years ago and who made a huge difference in my life and early speaking career. I reconnected with old neighbors, college friends, and two doctors who served with me on the Board of Northern Theological Seminary in Oak Brook, IL, before I moved to Florida in 2004. I even tracked down and spoke several times with an old boyfriend from my high school days!

Think about what small thing you can do for the next 100 (or 10 or 30) days to make a positive difference in some way. You could write one card or note a day or you could say a special prayer for one new person every day. Whatever you might choose, it will help you get beyond your feelings of loss, concentrate on someone else, and bring both of you special joy in a very difficult time.

Reminder checklist:

- Learn new things.
- Start a 100 Day Project.
- Each day contact someone who has been important in your life.

To download the checklists and other information, go to:

https://barbaraglanz.com/book-extras

Chapter Eight:
MALE PERSPECTIVES ON COPING MECHANISMS

WHEN I WORKED with a male colleague on some of this material, I found that his coping mechanisms were quite different from mine. Here are some of the things he found that helped him and others of his work colleagues as things changed in their work lives.

- **Separate areas of your life into "water-tight compartments."** He found that in order to cope during the struggle, he needed to keep different areas of his life separate—for example, his home life, his work life, and his spiritual life. That way he could deal with only one part of his life at a time by creating boundaries.

- **Maintain a strong work focus.** He felt that if he could focus on what he knew, his work, he did not become overwhelmed with the struggles in other aspects of his life. This kept his mind off his pain at least for part of his day.

- **Continue projects that provide continuity and complete projects that provide closure.** These familiar activities gave him a sense of control in areas he could manage and brought him satisfaction in the midst of so many painful things that were out of his control.

- **Perform activities that give you comfort and peace.** He found peace in familiar activities like playing golf, going to the gym, increasing social events, and attending church which all helped him cope.

- **Make logical assessments of the facts.** This is definitely a more male coping technique since feelings (human level) are much harder to handle for many men, so focusing on the facts (business level) seems to help some of them move forward.

The most important thing during this most difficult part of change is finding what works for you. Do not be influenced by anyone else if their methods are not comfortable for you. We each have to find our own way through this transition.

In her book, "Keep Moving," Maggie Smith reflects on finding optimism in the dark days following a collapsed marriage and other struggles. "Write 'breathe' on your to-do list," she advises. "Write 'blink.' Write 'sit and eat.' Then cross everything off. How satisfying! Give yourself credit for living." It's all about kindness, hope and why we need to keep moving, no matter what life hurls at us.

Reminder checklist:

- Separate areas of your life into "water-tight" compartments.
- Maintain a strong work focus.
- Continue projects that provide continuity and complete projects that provide closure.
- Perform activities that give you comfort and peace.
- Make logical assessments of the facts.

To download the checklists and other information, go to:

https://barbaraglanz.com/book-extras

Chapter Nine:
LETTING GO OF "WHAT WAS"

THIS IS THE most difficult stage of the whole change process but working though it will ultimately bring clarification and amazing growth as you discover what you need to let go of in your life in order to move forward. Although this stage takes time to accomplish, simply naming it is a start to the healing process.

For example, when our baby died, I had to let go of being a mother to this child and watching him grow and become an adult. I had to let go of feeling that I had done something wrong during my pregnancy. I had to let go of focusing on a future with two sons as planned.

When my husband died, I had to let go of my identity as a wife and part of a couple. I no longer fit with our couple friends, and they stopped inviting me to dinner parties and events. I had to learn to be a "young" widow and accept that I no longer had a partner in my life with whom to share things.

When I lost my job, I had to let go of the work relationships I had with all the trainers who had reported to me, and sadly, some of the friendships because of time and distance. I had to let go of the status and security of my job and the income I received.

Yet, in all these situations once I recognized, verbalized, and accepted what I had to let go of, I ultimately found new gifts to fill those gaps and add joy to my life. Unfortunately, many people are so focused on their losses that they hold onto the past, not letting go of "what was," and never move beyond this stage.

One of the best tools my colleague and I created to help us begin to reframe a change from something overwhelming to finding the gifts in it was the Control Inventory.

Chapter Ten:
THE CONTROL INVENTORY™

THIS CHART HAS been the most profound and yet simple example of what each of us has to answer in order to move through the changes in our lives. When you truly take time to think through these three questions with each change that occurs in your life, you will find a clarity which will allow you to discover the gifts from that change and free you to move forward.

First of all, name the situation and the actual change in your life. Then answer these three questions:

CONTROL INVENTORY™

The Situation (Change):

What do I have control over?	**What do I have no control over?**
What has changed in my life?	**What has not changed in my life?**

What do I have to let go of in order to move forward?

1. What do I have control over and what do I have no control over?

As you think about this question, I think you will realize that even though some things are out of your control, there are still many areas of your life in which you DO have control. Those are the areas you want to focus on.

When I was faced with the death of my child, I realized I had no control over what had happened, but I did have control over what I would do with the rest of my life. I could wallow in my grief or I could start, five minutes at a time, to pick up the pieces of my heart and be a wife to my husband and a mother to my remaining child. It was NOT easy and took a long time, but I finally succeeded and am a better person because of what I learned.

In the pandemic, for example, we do not have any control over the virus, but we have great control of our time and our interactions. We can wear our masks, socially distance and not choose to be in large crowds. We can do things outdoors that we once did inside. We can form our own "bubble" of close friends and family who are also sheltering, and we can get our flu shots and take our vitamins.

2. What has changed in my life and what has not changed in my life?

Again, as you ponder this question, I think you will find that even though something very significant may have changed in your life, there are many more things that have stayed the same.

When my child and husband died and when I lost a job I loved, I realized that even though circumstances in my life had changed drastically, I was still the same person with the same skills, the same values, and the same love for others. We can stew in what has changed or we can focus on what has not changed and find our way forward. Again, this is NOT easy, but it is a strong beginning to healing.

3. What do I have to let go of in order to move forward?

This is the most important and yet the most difficult question of all, and yet the answer is crucial in order for you to arrive at a new beginning. It will not be easy; however, you may remember the proverb that the beginning of wisdom is understanding. What I have found is that once you NAME what

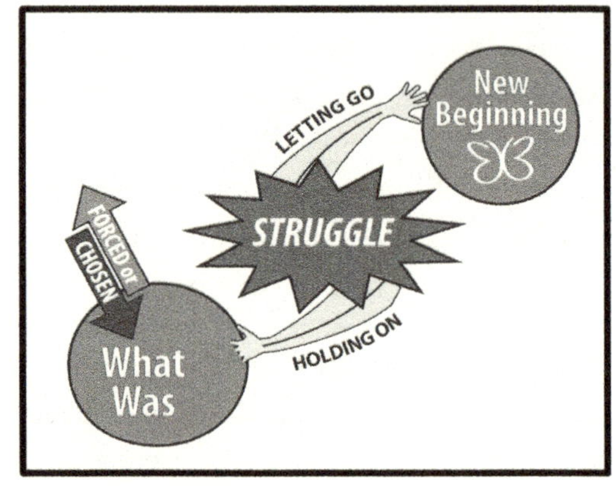

it is that you must let go of, you have gained understanding which leads to wisdom and the process of healing.

Go back to the model of change and now look at the hand that is holding onto "What Was." After any difficult change, our human level reaction is to hold onto the past.

> "Those were the good old days."
> "That is the way we have always done it."
> "If only …"
> "I cannot survive being alone."
> "I will never trust again."
> "I just want to return to 'normal'."
> "My life will never ever be the same without _________."

Unfortunately, many people never work through the struggle phase of change and spend the rest of their lives pining for or even living in the past.

Think for a moment about the monkey bars in the children's playground. We hold on tight, afraid of falling, but In order to move forward to the next bar, we have to let go of the one behind or we are stuck in the very same place forever.

When my husband died, as I mentioned earlier, I had to let go of my identity as a wife and part of a couple. I had to find a whole new group of single friends. When I moved to Florida, I had to let go of everything that was familiar and find new resources and new places to go with new people. After I lost my job, I had to let go of the financial and professional status of a management position and all those colleague and client relationships that were so important to me.

When it is a chosen change, it is somewhat easier to let go, but a forced change can take a long time for us to let go of the past and move forward. The pandemic was a forced change for all of us, so think about these three questions from the Control Inventory™ in terms of the changes you have experienced.

1. We do not have control over the virus, but we DO have control over wearing our masks, washing our hands, getting the vaccine, and social distancing. We have control over our votes for local, state, and national candidates who have responded either positively or negatively to the pandemic. We have control over how we use our time each day. What other things do you still have control over?

2. Many external things in our lives have changed, but there are still many things that have stayed the same during the pandemic— our friends, our families, our skills, our values. Even though you

may have lost your job or find yourself in brand new situations working or going to school at home, try to identify what has NOT changed in your life and be grateful for those things.

3. For each one of us, what we have to let go of will be different. And this is the hardest task to address. Yet, when we identify whatever it is we need to release, and accept as real, it becomes easier to do over time. For most of us during the pandemic, it has meant letting go of being with our friends and families, hugs and handshakes, going out to dinner, to church, to the movies, to sporting and arts events, even to school and our jobs. It may even have meant letting go of a job we love. We are left with insecurity and fear, so we desperately need to find the blessings in the midst of the change and realize that things will never be the same again. Yet, over time, the "new reality" may be even more fulfilling than the past. As long as we hold onto the past and the "way it was," however, we will never be able to move to a new beginning and find out.

One of the most exciting things about this whole transition process is that even in the midst of the pain, this can be our most creative period. As we discover new coping tools and find new ways of viewing our lives, amazing things can happen.

The highest levels of integration come after the
highest levels of disruption.

~Ian Percy

Conclusion:
FINDING THE GIFTS IN A NEW BEGINNING

The most beautiful people we have known are those who have known defeat, known suffering, known struggle, known loss, and have found their way out of the depths. These persons have an appreciation, a sensitivity, and an understanding of life that fills them with compassion, gentleness, and a deep loving concern. Beautiful people do not just happen.

~Elizabeth Kubler Ross

AT THIS STAGE you are finally accepting that the change has occurred and are beginning to think about the future. You have realized that you do have control over many things in your life, and that although a huge change may have taken place, there are still many things that have not changed. And most important of all, you have named and worked on what you have to let go of in order to move to a new beginning.

This process may take weeks, months or even years, and sometimes we may just want to go back to "What Was." However, if we do not work through this process on the human level, we will never grow and find new ways to live our lives.

The tough news is that we are going to have to go through this process again and again on a larger or smaller scale for the rest of our lives since change is inevitable in our world today. Learning to understand the process itself and developing your own coping mechanisms will be crucial to a more balanced and fulfilling life.

You WILL survive … yet finding peace and joy and the gifts in the growth process is your choice. Some of the gifts I found from the changes in my life have been the following:

1. **Redefined priorities**—Pain and loss have helped me learn what is truly important in my life. For example, I have learned that all material things in my life can be taken away in a moment. The only things that are lasting are the relationships I have. This has made me examine where I put the bulk of my time and energy—on working and being successful in my profession or on the people for whom I care. I choose people!

2. **New and Deeper Relationships**—Everyone has a story and hearing mine and the process I struggled through often creates a bond that allows others to be honest and free to share their struggles as well. I strongly believe that we admire others for their strengths, but we love them for their vulnerabilities because that makes them human, just like us! When we have gone through trials of any kind, we

become much more empathetic and compassionate, and we can end up helping others in similar situations. We truly can say, "I understand your pain."

3. **Depth of Character**—In the midst of the most devastating changes in my life, I realized that no one could ever hurt me as much as I was already hurting, so I made the decision that I would always be my true authentic self and not be influenced by trying to please others or worry about what they thought of me. That decision has made a huge difference in my life, and it has made me not be afraid to be vulnerable. As I share my struggles with my audiences either through speaking or writing, it causes me to realize how blessed I really am. I am truly grateful for the challenges and losses in my life as they have molded me into the person I am today.

4. **More Joy and Fulfillment in Life**—I have always loved a quote from "The Prophet" by Kahlil Gibran. He says that the deeper sorrow carves into our being, we have that much more capacity to experience joy. That thought has blessed me many times because I realize that people who might only have had small sorrows in their lives will probably not have very significant joys either. However, those of us who have suffered through deep pain, can, if we choose, also have deep joy in our lives. I think we appreciate that joy even more because of our struggle. That is one of the most precious gifts change can bring!

I would ask you one final question. Remember the quotation I used earlier, "**All change comes bearing gifts?**" Look back on the changes in your life and if you are willing, write down the gift(s) that came with each of them. When you able to do that, it becomes the ultimate place of healing. I wish you a hope-filled and stretching journey as you discover the many lasting GIFTS that can come though Change.

Blessings,

We are blessed by beginnings and endings.
The circle takes us away from and then back to our origin.
So endings are beginnings and beginnings are endings. The one requires
the other.
The Sufis greet sudden disappointment with joy. Loss signals the
beginning of new growth.
We can do this.
It requires letting go.
To let loss or failure trigger letting go is the gift, our spiritual challenge.
But what a blessing when we admit defeat, loss, new wisdom replacing
old.
For the seeker, loss is only a beginning.
We only lose when we fail to begin.
Winners are beginners.

~John MacEnulty

ACKNOWLEDGEMENTS

Special thanks goes to my friend, Mike, who years ago helped me design the workshop that inspired this book. Also, I want to share my deepest appreciation for my longtime assistant, Laura Roberts, who keeps me organized and acts as my sounding board and encourager; Gianna Peralli, who keeps my social networking sites up-to-date; my wonderful MasterMind group, John, Jolene, Bev, and Barry, and finally, Randy Gawlik, my webmaster, son-in-love, and the one who always "bails us out" when we have computer problems. Finally, a huge debt of gratitude goes to my new friend, photographer Joseph Coulombe, who so generously allowed me to use his sunrise photograph of Siesta Key, the beach where I live, as my cover. I feel so very blessed to have these precious people in my life.

ABOUT THE AUTHOR

A member of the prestigious Speaker Hall of Fame, Barbara Glanz, CSP, CPAE, works with organizations to improve morale, retention and service and with individuals who want to rediscover joy and purpose in their lives. She is the first speaker on record to have spoken **on all 7 continents and in all 50 states.**

Known as "the business speaker who speaks to your heart as well as to your head," Barbara is the author of fourteen books including ***The Simple Truths of Service Inspired by Johnny the Bagger®,*** co-authored with Ken Blanchard, ***CARE Packages for the Workplace***, and ***180 Ways to Spread Contagious Enthusiasm™***. She is known for her inspiring presentations on **Employee Engagement, Customer Service, Appreciation & Recognition, Change,** and **Kindness.**

Voted **"best keynote presenter you have heard or used"** by Meetings & Conventions Magazine, Barbara uses her Master's degree in Adult Learning to design programs that cause behavior change, and she guarantees that her audience members will leave with at least 6-8 immediately applicable, no-cost action ideas. She lives and breathes her personal motto, "Spreading Contagious Enthusiasm™.

She can be reached at bglanz@barbaraglanz.com or
www.barbaraglanz.com.

Made in the USA
Monee, IL
18 December 2021